Living
Evangelization

Series Preface

The volumes in NCP's "7 x 4" series offer a meditation a day for four weeks, a bite of food for thought, a reflection that lets a reader ponder the spiritual significance of each and every day. Small enough to slip into a purse or coat pocket, these books fit easily into everyday routines.

Living Evangelization

Three Minute Reflections on Faith

Joan Mueller

New City Press
Hyde Park, New York

Published in the United States by New City Press
202 Comforter Blvd., Hyde Park, NY 12538
www.newcitypress.com
©2012 Joan Mueller

Cover design by Durva Correia

Library of Congress Cataloging-in-Publication Data

Mueller, Joan, 1956-
  Living evangelization : three minute reflections on faith / Joan Mueller.
    p. cm.
  ISBN 978-1-56548-456-6 (alk. paper)
  1. Catholic Church--Doctrines--Meditations. I. Title.
  BX2182.3.M84 2012
  242--dc23
                        2012017610

Printed in the United States of America

Contents

one

The Gift of Faith

two

Our Faith Conversion

three

Mary, Model of Faith

four

Our Evangelizing Mission

Introduction

A blustery wind rattled the rickety windows of the inner city church sacristy, while a group of Sudanese refugees and I huddled against the cold. We were completing the reflections required for parents preparing to celebrate the baptism of their babies, and these parents were looking forward eagerly to next Sunday's celebrations. I had taken time to prepare the process for the day. We would examine the theme of love by reading the parable of the lost sheep. The lesson of the story is, of course, obvious. God loves each of us so much that even if we stray, God will leave the ninety-nine in order to find the one who is lost. God loves each of us, uniquely and unconditionally. No matter how we might stray, God will seek us out.

We began reading the parable, and the parents listened with acute attentiveness. They loved hearing the scripture read aloud, since reading and celebrating their faith was often punished in Southern Sudan where churches were burned, villages destroyed, and Christians imprisoned and tortured. I learned many things from those newcomers to American life, perhaps most importantly, how to reverence and cherish the reading of the scriptures.

After the reading, I asked a simple question: "What message do you think God wants us to hear in this text?" Presuming that the answer would be some variation on God's love and care, I had the rest of the process outlined.

One of the men answered. "It's about faith," he said. Others in the group nodded in affirmation. Taken aback, but not wanting to betray my surprise, I simply asked why he thought it was about faith. In reply he offered not a metaphysical response but a story.

"When I was in Southern Sudan," he said, "the enemy came to my village. They captured me, and threw me in chains into a dark room. They made me sleep on damp concrete for one year. The soldiers would come and put electricity through me, and ask me if I was a Christian. Many times I thought they would stop if I denied my faith, but God gave me courage. No matter what they did to me, I said: 'I am a Christian.' Finally, they became tired and let me go. I am alive; I am free because I said, 'I am a Christian.'"

As I listened, I realized that these people were looking at the parable of the lost sheep from an entirely different perspective — the perspective of faith. While I interpreted the parable as a love story, they perceived it as a faith story. It was their story — they were lost, tortured, alone, forgotten, and now were free. The birth and baptism of their babies was an exuberant celebration of new life that came from this persevering faith.

Opening the celebration of the fiftieth anniversary of the Second Vatican Council, Pope Benedict XVI's apostolic letter, *The Door of Faith*, invites Christians to reflect on their gift of faith. This book will use passages from *The Door of Faith* in order to focus our reflections. Over the course of four weeks, we will ponder our faith perspective, our faith conversion, Mary as a model of our faith, and our mission of faith. Like those Sudanese parents, it is hoped that pondering our Christian experience of faith might bring us new vision, new courage, new joy, and a profound sense of living faith in action.

To use this book, pray through the exercises day by day. Each day has a scripture passage, a passage from The Door of Faith, a reflection, and a spiritual practice. If you choose to pray the book over the course of a month, use one exercise daily. You might also choose to move more slowly, spending more than one day on spiritual practices that need a little more time. Enjoy the journey, and let us pray for each other!

The Gift
of Faith

1 Reflecting on the Beginnings of Our Faith

When Paul and Barnabas arrived, they called the church together and related all that God had done with them, and how he had opened a door of faith for the Gentiles.

Acts 14:27

The door of faith is always open for us, ushering us into a life of communion with God.

The Door of Faith, 1

Just imagine how happy Paul and Barnabas were to return to Antioch after their two-year missionary journey. There, the well-established Christian community had been praying for the two of them as they preached the Good News throughout Asia Minor. Paul's report of their journey was stunning — Gentiles were listening and considering his message seriously.

In the Hellenized cities that Paul and Barnabas visited, the inhabitants had their own folk gods and goddesses as well as established Jewish synagogues. Even more importantly, they had astute and sophisticated philosophies. In Asia Minor, the novel message of Jesus had to compete with the time-honored, traditional writings of Plato, Socrates, and Aristotle.

Given this, it is not surprising that Paul and Barnabas were elated, even though their mission had limited success in terms of actual converts. Through their preaching, Jesus, an outlier from Judea, was now in dialogue with the Greek philosophical world. He had gained a hearing — the door of faith was opened.

Spiritual Practice

Try to remember when you first were invited to consider belief in God. Did you experience this gift of faith in your family, among friends, through a church outreach program? Did a particular event prod you to open yourself to belief?

Today, spend some time recalling the beginnings of your faith. Whether weak or strong, your faith had a beginning. To become strong in faith, it is good to reflect upon and be grateful for this beginning. As you recall where and how your faith journey began, ask God to bless all those who fostered your belief, who taught you, and who encouraged you.

2   Pondering our Faith Journey

Now faith is the assurance of things hoped for, the conviction of things not seen. By faith Abraham obeyed when he was called to set out for a place that he was to receive as an inheritance; and he set out, not knowing where he was going. For he looked forward to the city that has foundations, whose architect and builder is God.

Hebrews 11:1,8,10

To enter through the door of faith is to set out on a journey that lasts a lifetime.

Door of Faith 1

Human life requires belief. If I drive a car, I need to believe that other drivers, for the most part, will stay in their lanes and obey the rules of the road. If I decide to get married, I am entering into a life of faith with another person. Marriage is indeed a leap of faith. On their wedding day, neither bride nor groom can prove that their relationship will last a lifetime. They can only make the leap of faith, believing and hoping that their marriage vows will endure. This trust, this faith in another person can be realized only day by day, year by year.

Like Abraham of old, at some point we began a pilgrimage of faith and to some extent our lives have been shaped by that decision. Like Abraham, our journeys through life have brought us good days and bad, times of doubt and times of joy. We have rejoiced in our faith and have also been confused and discouraged. These ups and downs are typical of all relationships, even of our relationship with God.

Spiritual Practice

"How sad," a Franciscan friar was fond of saying, "that so many of us walk alone when God is begging to walk through life with us." As you consider your life of faith today, have you been conscious of walking with God, or have you, for the most part, walked alone? When has God been most present in your life?

Now, imagine putting together a scrapbook of memories of your faith journey with God. What would be the important moments of this journey? What pictures does your mind's eye place on each page? What would be the high points of your faith journey? What would be the moments of sadness or discouragement?

As you look to the next steps in your faith journey, how might you be more conscious of the presence of God? "How sad that so many of us walk alone, when God is begging to walk through life with us!"

3 Appreciating our Baptismal Dignity

When you were buried with Christ in baptism, you were also raised with him through faith in the power of God, who raised him from the dead.

Colossians 2:12

The journey of faith begins with baptism.

Door of Faith 1

Seldom do western Christians reflect upon the mystery of their baptism. This is odd, since faith is based in our union with the death and resurrection of Jesus celebrated in baptism. In baptism, Paul says, we are buried and raised with Christ. Instead of patterning our behavior around religious laws and regulations, Christians are to live in union with Jesus, who died and now lives with God in glory.

To be buried with Christ, we must do our best to change behaviors not befitting the heavenly inheritance promised at our baptism. Do we curse, gossip, steal, betray, commit sexual infidelities, cheat, or complain? None of these actions are becoming to those who belong to the family of God. In baptism, we are reborn into God's family, into the dynamic love that is Father, Son, and Holy Spirit. We experience this love and, in return, are called to love God, others, and self.

Spiritual Practice

In baptism, you were reborn as an adopted son or daughter of God and were raised up to participate in loving Trinitarian relationships. As you consider this today, think about how well you fit into the family of God. Does your behavior and demeanor reflect your dignity? What behaviors might you change or improve to mirror more fully the divine dignity that is yours?

While there are behaviors and attitudes that we might change, there are also weaknesses that overwhelm us and make us feel helpless. Are we addicted to a substance or negative action? Do we worry too much? Are we unable to relax or ask others for help? Do we find ourselves gossiping even after we have decided not to? If this is the case, place yourself before God's presence and ask for the grace you need. Do all you can to change and, for the rest, rely on the effective action of God in your life.

Finally, try to imagine yourself "on the other side," in the heavenly presence. Because God is love, God's presence is healing and forgiving. Stay in God's presence and, with the eyes of faith, ask for healing and mercy. Then, as you go about your day, try to extend this same love and mercy to others.

4 Imagining our Faith Transformed in Glory

He was destined before the foundation of the world, but was revealed at the end of the ages for your sake. Through him you have come to trust in God, who raised him from the dead and gave him glory, so that your faith and hope are set on God.

1 Peter 1:20-21

The journey of faith ends with the passage through death to eternal life, fruit of the resurrection of the Lord Jesus, whose will it was, by the gift of the Holy Spirit, to draw those who believe in him into his own glory.

The Door of Faith 1

Christians believe in God because of Jesus Christ. It is Christ who is our way, truth, and life, our path to God, our contemplation of the glory of God. When Christians think about their faith journey, they realize that they learned of divinity not through philosophical abstractions, but through the person of Jesus Christ, fully human and fully divine. Because of his humanity, Christ became one of us and left us an example to follow. Because of his divinity, Christ reconciles us with heavenly glory and permits us, through grace, to partake in the divine life of God.

As Christians we believe intellectually in God, but we also believe that we join Jesus Christ in his death and resurrection. Because death could not hold down the glorious divinity of Christ, we, who are joined to Christ in baptism, also break out of the tomb to be united with Jesus in glory.

Spiritual Exercise

When face to face with death, we realize the faith it takes to confront it with the hope that something is waiting for us on the other side. We know what we have here—our family, friends, work, professional life — but we have no idea what awaits us once we pass. We hope, perhaps, that after death we will be met by loved ones who have gone before us and who, in a sense, will show us how to live in a resurrected world, a world imbued with God's glory.

Today, imagine what the next world might be like. How do you think God will look upon you? What kind of respect would God show others who are with you? Would God welcome all people, or just some? Is the axiom: "The love of God is the love of neighbor" lived in your image of heaven? What does this love of neighbor look like?

5 Mirroring the Love of God and Neighbor

By this we know that we abide in him and he in us, because he has given us of his Spirit.

And we have seen and do testify that the Father has sent his Son as the Savior of the world. God abides in those who confess that Jesus is the Son of God, and they abide in God. So we have known and believe the love that God has for us. God is love, and those who abide in love abide in God, and God abides in them.

1 John 4:13-16

To profess faith in the Trinity — Father, Son and Holy Spirit — is to believe in one God who is Love.

The Door of Faith 1

Christians believe that God is three persons — Father, Son, and Holy Spirit — in one divine nature. While all believers learned this in a religion class somewhere, few, perhaps, have ever really considered the profundity of this belief for our adult faith. Why is belief in the Trinitarian God important for Christians?

We have reflected that we are invited into our Christian faith journey through baptism and that this journey culminates in our resurrection with Christ in glory. Our understanding of faith is made possible because God sent his Son into the world to be for us the way, the truth, and the life. Through Jesus' death and resurrection we become adopted sons and daughters in Christ. This means that we are adopted into the divinity of God — we are divinized by God's gift of grace.

The early church fathers said: "God became human, so that human beings could become divine." Of course, unlike Jesus Christ, we are not divine by nature. We are human beings. It is through the death and resurrection of Jesus Christ that we are adopted into the Trinitarian family — Father, Son, and Holy Spirit … and us!

Spiritual Exercise

In your reflection today, imagine God as the loving union of Father, Son, and Holy Spirit. Thinking back to your baptism, consider God's invitation to you as a child of God adopted through grace by Jesus Christ. Imagine yourself truly within the Trinitarian family relating with the Father, Son, and Holy Spirit.

Next, reflect upon the fact that those with whom you live and work are also invited to be adopted sons and daughters of Christ. Of course to be a true family, the love that the Father, Son, and Holy Spirit are giving you must be mirrored in your love and care for others. "God is love, and those who abide in love abide in God, and God abides in them" (1 John 4:16).

Listening to God's Word as Truth

Sanctify them in the truth; your word is truth. As you have been sent me into the world, so I have sent them into the world.

John 17:17-18

By their very existence in the world, Christians are called to radiate the word of truth that the Lord Jesus Christ has left us.

The Door of Faith 6

"What is truth?" Pilate cynically asked Jesus, right before handing him over to be crucified. The Gospel of John answers that question: "Your word is truth." Truth comes from the word of God, which is an expression of the divine being.

Given this, we should not think about divine truth as a list of do's and don'ts listed in some sort of divine checklist! We can learn the truth, we can live a wise and holy life, only if we listen attentively to the living Word of God. God speaks the truth to us as we live and work in the world.

Some people confuse truth and law. They come up with a series of precepts and claim to have "God in a box." They have a religious answer for everything because their truth is from the law rather than from God. Jesus sends Christians into the world not with a catalogue of ready-made answers but with a mandate to listen and discern God's living Word in the midst of the world. Our faith is not based upon law, but upon our living relationship with the person of Jesus Christ.

Spiritual Exercise

Identify your deepest consolation in life. Is it your wife or husband offering unconditional love? Do your children bring you endless joy? Are you devoted to a charity or good work that gives meaning and wonder to your life? Are you a single person struggling to make a difference in the world?

Next try to identify the most challenging situation in your life right now. Why do you find this situation so difficult? What would have to change to make this circumstance easier to bear?

Finally, place both situations before God in prayer and ask for a response. God promises to journey with us and, within the complexities of our world, to speak the divine truth, which is always simple. Is your sense of consolation confirmed? Do you receive a suggestion regarding your difficulties? Allow God's Word to advise you and then return to the world putting that Word into practice.

Our Faith
Conversion

1 Bringing Heaven to Earth

But if we have died with Christ, we believe that we will also live with him. We know that Christ, being raised from the dead, will never die again; death no longer has dominion over him. The death he died, he died to sin, once for all; but the life he lives, he lives to God. So you also must consider yourselves dead to sin and alive to God in Christ Jesus.

Romans 6:8-11

In the mystery of his death and resurrection, God has revealed in its fullness the Love that saves and calls us to conversion of life.

Door of Faith 6

When my mother learned that her cancer was end-stage and she was going to die, she said to me: "Be patient with me, Joan, because I've never done this before." All of her life she had been a Catholic, had recited the words of the creed, and had been active in her small-town parish. Now that she was facing death, she realized that her lifelong belief was centered in her hope of resurrected life. What would the next life be like? Would she make the transition gracefully? Who would be there to meet her on the other side? Would she enjoy her new home in heaven even while her husband and children were still alive and well on earth?

In this age of medical miracles, death often seems far off. Meditating on death seems bizarre, even macabre. Yet death and the contemplation of life after death is core to the Christian message. The resurrection of Christ, the Easter season, is the high point of our Christian calendar. One could say that it is faith and hope in the resurrection that defines our life as Christians.

Spiritual Exercise

Today, imagine what the moment after your death might be like. What is your Christian hope? Will others be meeting you and introducing you to your new home? How will you feel about being there? Do you believe that you will rise again in Christ? What will God be like?

As you go about your day today, take the peace of heaven with you. As you meet others, try to remain in this peace, gently including them in your heavenly home.

2 Cooperating with Grace

I appeal to you therefore, brothers and sisters, by the mercies of God, to present your bodies as a living sacrifice, holy and acceptable to God, which is your spiritual worship. Do not be conformed to this world, but be transformed by the renewing of your minds, so that you may discern what is the will of God — what is good and acceptable and perfect.

Romans 12:1-2

To the extent that we freely cooperate, our thoughts and affections, mentality and conduct are slowly purified and transformed on a journey that is never completely finished in this life.

Door of Faith 6

When we think of conversion, we think of pain. Giving up smoking, for instance, brings about fears of withdrawal, weight gain, and the loss of one's smoking buddies. Only when the positives outweigh these negatives might a person try to change his or her behavior. If I start thinking about better health, more money in my wallet and a wider variety of friends, then I might be able to change my behavior. Even with such incentives, however, change is hard. It sometimes seems impossible.

This applies even more to behaviors that seem intrinsic to our characters. I would stop gossiping, but I don't even realize that I'm doing it. I would not get so upset, but my nerves just seem to take over. I would not become so angry, but I explode before I even realize I'm upset. Sometimes we feel helpless before these behaviors even though we would like very much to change.

Spiritual Exercise

Today list two behaviors that you would like to change in order to make you a better Christian. What holds you back? When are people surprised by your behavior? When do others become upset with you? Does your need for control smother others' freedom? Do you have a violent or aggressive streak? Do you dissolve in tears rather than face challenges? Do you always take the easy way out?

Next, think of one thing you might do to counter this tendency — don't try to cure it, just think about doing one small thing to act against it. Obviously, if it was easy to cure this tendency you would have done it already! Rather, we must counter the things that challenge us one action, one behavior at a time.

Finally, as Christians we believe that grace helps us in our weakness. Ask God to help you with your weakness. If you do one small thing, trust that God will support you in your efforts. In this, work as if everything depended upon you, and pray as though everything depended on God.

3 Praying for our Neighbor

As God's chosen ones, holy and beloved, clothe yourselves with compassion, kindness, humility, meekness, and patience. Bear with one another and, if anyone has a complaint against another, forgive each other; just as the Lord has forgiven you, so you also must forgive. Above all, clothe yourselves with love, which binds everything together in perfect harmony.

Colossians 3:12-14

Faith working through love becomes a new criterion of understanding and action that changes the whole of human life.

Door of Faith 6

You do not struggle with your weaknesses alone; every personality has its challenges. That neighbor who is always denigrating people maybe has a hard time appreciating herself. Perhaps that boss who never has a good word to say is fearful for his job. The colleague who is always dumping work on you might not be feeling well. While we can ponder the sources of our own challenges to virtue, we do not always know the story behind our neighbor's problematic behavior.

For small children, the world revolves around them. As we grow older, we realize that we may not have outgrown such a perception. We think that others act in response to our character—we take what they do to us as a personal affront. We try to change the negative behavior of others, but often our techniques don't work. We become frustrated because we can't control the situation, can't make our neighbor see things as we do.

Spiritual Exercise

Today, in someone you meet regularly, identify a behavior that really drives you crazy. Is your father-in-law always negative? Is your boss an egotistical bore? Do your children fail to appreciate you? Is your neighbor always disregarding your property line?

Next, consider why this behavior, in fact, is probably not about you. Perhaps your father-in-law suffers from depression that he hasn't come to accept. Maybe your boss feels insecure because he has been promoted beyond his competence. Perhaps your children are busy with their own responsibilities. Maybe your neighbor's anger stems from an affront from times gone by, and you are an easy target for it.

When others' lack of virtue caused Jesus to suffer, he prayed: "Father, forgive them; for they do not know what they are doing." When you meet frustration today, repeat that prayer with Jesus. Remember that "they do not know what they are doing." Their behavior may well not be about you. Rather than assessing blame, realize the others' weakness and pray for them.

5 Courting the Joy of Endless Tomorrows

But in your hearts sanctify Christ as Lord. Always be ready to make your defense to anyone who demands from you an accounting for the hope that is in you, yet do it with gentleness and reverence.

1 Peter 3:15

Faith makes us fruitful, because it expands our hearts in hope and enables us to bear life-giving witness.

Doors of Faith 7

By placing their faith in a resurrected life, Christians receive a great gift. No matter what happens, no matter what tragedy or suffering, they have hope. This is not an excuse for not working to make the present better, but when such improvement does not come about, hope sustains us.

Hope for a better world filled Jesus' preaching. Jesus knew the story in the book of Maccabees (2 Mc 7:1-42) of the woman who was forced to watch as a foreign enemy killed her seven sons because they refused to deny the practices of their Jewish faith and worship Greek gods. The family persevered because they believed in God's covenant of everlasting life. They welcomed their martyrdom with peace and perseverance, because they hoped in the resurrection.

During Jesus' time such belief in a future life was popular among the Pharisees, but the Sadducees, the priests who ran the Jewish Temple, rejected it. Persecutors consider belief in the resurrection dangerous because it diminishes their power. As long as the persecuted have hope, they are able to triumph over evil — not through force, but through the witness of their moral courage.

Those who believe in a resurrected life need not be militants. They do not hope in a cause, but in God. Because of this, they can take radical stands without raising their voices. They can make their defense to anyone who demands from them an accounting for the hope that is in them, yet do it with gentleness and reverence.

Spiritual Exercise

Live today as though you had endless tomorrows. Because you are not bound by time, relax. Go with the flow. If stuck in traffic, enjoy some music. If rushed, breathe deeply and slow yourself down. If insulted or snubbed, remind yourself that you are deeply loved by others and by God.

In the midst of these endless tomorrows, court joy. Since you have no need to become worried or upset, notice the colors of the leaves, the beauty on the faces of children, the glory of the morning sky. As you walk the world today, try to allow you heart to expand and bring your joy of life into your world.

Surrendering into the Hands of God

Then Jesus, crying with a loud voice, said, "Father, into your hands I commend my spirit." Having said this, he breathed his last. When the centurion saw what had taken place, he praised God and said, "Certainly this man was innocent."

Luke 23:46-47

There is no possibility for certitude regarding one's life other than ever-growing self-abandonment into the hands of a love that grows constantly because its origin is in God.

Door of Faith 7

Once, when I lived in Milwaukee, I was coming home from work on a city bus. At a downtown stop, a Vietnamese man, by his appearance a refugee, came aboard. Instead of just finding a seat, he repeated under his breath, just audibly enough for everyone to hear, "damn, damn, damn." It struck me, as well as others on the bus, as quite funny because although the man could not speak much English, he had picked up this rather unfortunate expletive. He must have heard others speakers using this same turn of phrase and picked it up in an attempt to acculturate — to be an American.

When someone hurts us, we often swear spontaneously. The words are out before we even think. When our children pick this habit up, we nervously backtrack, trying to explain to them why we may have cursed, but they should not.

When Jesus died on the cross, he had every reason to curse. He was innocent of the charges. He was a religiously observant man and did not deserve the death sentence. He was God ...

Rather than curse, however, with his last breath Jesus placed himself into the hands of the Father. The next time that Luke mentions Jesus' spirit is at Pentecost. And what does God do with Jesus' spirit? The Spirit forms the church and encourages the very apostles who had abandoned and denied Jesus.

Spiritual Exercise

As we grow older, or if we become ill, we realize that there is a lot in our lives that we cannot control. At these times, we have two choices. We can curse our fate and those we might hold responsible for our misfortune, or we can surrender our lives into the hands of God. Cursing might bring momentary release, but Jesus gave us a clear example of how to respond to suffering.

Reflect on when you might be tempted to curse in your life. Offer this suffering to God using the prayer of Jesus. When memories of this suffering surface, or when a swear word slips, try to repeat Jesus' prayer, "Into your hands, Lord, I commend my spirit."

7 Examining our Following

The Lord looks down from heaven on humankind to see if there are any who are wise, who seek after God.

Psalm 14:2

Simply knowing what to believe is not sufficient unless this knowledge is joined by a heart opened by grace that allows the eyes to see below the surface and to understand that what has been proclaimed is the Word of God.

Door of Faith 10

Knowledge is power. If we manage to learn chemical compounds and pass required exams, we might find that the state will give us the power to practice pharmacy. If we manage to learn and interpret the law and again, pass the required exams, we may be given the authority to represent others in a court of law. If we understand what makes another person tick, we may find that we can manipulate the other or love the other better — according to our choice.

A TV preacher used to introduce himself with all his credentials, including the number of hours in his life that he had studied and read the Bible. How could a person even calculate this! He sub-

stantiated some rather outrageous claims concern-
ing the second coming of Christ by appealing to
his store of knowledge. He expected his viewers
to believe his predictions because he claimed to
have spent a great deal of time studying.

God is beloved in our lives — not a subject to
be studied, but a mystery to be appreciated and
cherished. We might learn about God by studying theology, but we come to know God only by
"faith seeking understanding." In other words,
whatever we might learn about God is insuffi-
cient. Although learning facts might give us some
insights, we can understand God only in loving
relationship. If we study God's word, we might
receive information. If, however, we listen and
cherish the beloved word of God, we have the
potential to become wise.

Spiritual Exercise

Reflect today on those in your life whom you
have followed spiritually. Why have you followed
them? Why have you believed them? Do you
believe because they wield institutional power?
Do you trust them because their credentials have
dazzled you? Have these decisions been good for
you?

Now, imagine yourself to be a first-century
person who is following Jesus. Why would you
follow him? What kind of credentials does he offer? What makes him attractive to you?

Mary, Model of Faith

three

Welcoming God's Courtesy

And he came to her and said, "Greetings, favored one! The Lord is with you." But she was much perplexed by his words and pondered what sort of greeting this might be. The angel said to her, "Do not be afraid, Mary, for you have found favor with God. And now, you will conceive in your womb and bear a son, and you will name him Jesus. He will be great, and will be called the Son of the Most High, and the Lord God will give to him the throne of his ancestor David.

Then Mary said, "Here am I, the servant of the Lord; let it be with me according to your word." Then the angel departed from her.

Luke 1:28-32; 38

By faith, Mary accepted the angel's word and believed the message that she was to become the Mother of God.

Door of Faith 13

In her writings the English mystic, Julian of Norwich, maintains that God is courteous. Perhaps no scripture passage better illustrates God's courtesy than the story of the annunciation. Mary hears the angel's announcement and is afraid — of course! She has questions — she asks the angel how a virgin can have a child. God allows Mary, a woman of lowly birth, to think about the plan that the angel has described and respond freely. God, who has every right over creatures, courteously waits for a human woman's consent to this request.

Mary could have said "No." Had she done so, God would have accepted her answer and turned to another plan of salvation, one that would also have respected human freedom. Mary's "yes," however, invited God to become human so that we could share in divine life. God's courtesy gave her the freedom to pronounce a "yes" that welcomed divine grace in a free, generous act of love.

Spiritual Exercise

As you ponder the mystery of Mary's annunciation, imagine what the angel Gabriel might say if he appeared to you. In your life right now, what is God asking of you? How are you responding to God's courteous invitation? If you have not said "yes," address God, as Mary did, with the questions that prevent you from doing so. What does God say about these obstacles?

Many times God's will for our lives seems inconsequential. We take care of a loved one who is ill. We make our children their lunches every day. We clean the house and take out the garbage.

Ponder the everydayness of Mary's "yes." While we see the annunciation as a dramatic event, the reality of Mary's life was also making meals, tending to a child, and cleaning the house. Renew your dedication to your daily tasks, knowing that your generous response reveals divine love working on earth.

2 Dreaming God's Dream

And Mary said, "My soul magnifies the Lord, and my spirit rejoices in God my Savior, for he has looked with favor on the lowliness of his servant. Surely, from now on all generations will call me blessed…. He has shown strength with his arm; he has scattered the proud in the thoughts of their hearts. He has brought down the powerful from their thrones, and lifted up the lowly; he has filled the hungry with good things, and sent the rich away empty.

Luke 1:46-48, 51-53

Visiting Elizabeth, she raised her hymn of praise to the Most High for the marvels worked in those who trust God.

Door of Faith 13

Mary's Magnificat is a radical prayer. God's gaze falls upon a lowly woman and she carries the divine child. She describes the revolutionary consequences of this event, unique in human history: the proud are confused, their plans and plots unraveled, their powerful connections broken. Kings are dethroned and peasants assume a new dignity. Rich fare is set before the hungry, while the stomachs of the rich growl.

Both Mary and Elizabeth, two ordinary pregnant women, knew that the life within them was miraculous. Both welcomed this miracle and rejoiced in it. Each understood that her child would become more than she could ever be, and marveled at this gift of God. Both sensed the wonder of grace and peace that their children would bring to the world.

Spiritual Exercise

Mary and Elizabeth each saw her child from God's perspective. They understood that the lives growing within them were God's gift, that God had a plan for these children. As you ponder Mary's visit to Elizabeth, think about the times in your own life that filled you with joy, when you were truly happiest. What qualities filled these moments — relationship, accomplishment, quiet? When are you most at-home with your true, happy self?

Reflecting on such moments of happiness, look at the life you are living right now. Are you happy? Are you responding to God's call? Are you the person God created you to be? If not, ponder what you need to change to renew God's dream for you. Decide which small step to take today toward becoming the gift God created you to be.

3 Fixing Your Eyes Into God's

While they were there in Bethlehem, the time came for her to deliver her child. And she gave birth to her firstborn son and wrapped him in bands of cloth, and laid him in a manger, because there was no place for them in the inn.

Luke 2:6-7

With joy and trepidation, Mary gave birth to her only son.

Door of Faith 13

They were on a journey that had been difficult enough when St. Teresa of Avila and her companions came upon a swollen, raging river. There was no bridge. Looking up, Teresa fixed her eyes toward heaven and said: "If this is the way you treat your friends, it's no wonder you have so few of them!"

In the Christmas story, Mary is pregnant with the son of God. One would expect that God would provide at least first-century basic care. She should have been at home with a midwife nearby, eagerly waiting the birth of her baby. Instead, she is on the road far from home, in a strange city without family or friends.

When Joseph and Mary finally arrived at the inn, there wasn't a room to be had. In the end, Mary gave birth to God's son in a barn and wrapped him — not in handmade linens made by the neighbor women — but in rags perhaps torn from Joseph's own clothes. Mary, too, might have fixed her eyes on the heavens and said, "If this is the way you treat your friends, it's no wonder you have so few of them!"

But having a child changes everything. Mary is a bit anxious, but also excited, happy, elated. Obeying God brings both trouble and joy.

Spiritual Exercise

Following God's call doesn't always bring about admiration. In fact, obeying God, most likely, will bring us trouble and pain. We too might shake our finger at God like St. Teresa and say, "If this is the way you treat your friends, it's no wonder you have so few of them."

Our lives are made happiest, however, not through worldly accomplishments. Often the happiest moments are our quietest periods of faithful relationship or of self-giving generosity.

If we focus on the trouble and forget the happiness, we get stuck. Today, focus on the happiness in your life and be grateful for all that God has given you.

4 Making Peace with Our Exile

An angel of the Lord appeared to Joseph in a dream and said, "Get up, take the child and his mother, and flee to Egypt, and remain there until I tell you; for Herod is about to search for the child, to destroy him."

Then Joseph got up, took the child and his mother by night, and went to Egypt, and remained there until the death of Herod.

Matthew 2:13-15

Trusting her husband, Joseph, Mary took Jesus to Egypt to save him from Herod's persecution.

Door of Faith 13

A few years ago, I received a call from a local hospital. A child had broken his leg and his mother, one of the Sudanese with whom I was working, was hysterical. The doctors had stabilized the child, but the mother was still beside herself. Could I come to the hospital and help?

When I arrived, the nurses gave the mom and me a private room. She was still crying uncontrollably, and I held her for a long time. Finally, through her sobs, she spoke. In the Sudan, a compound fracture like the one that her son had sustained meant certain death. When soldiers had burned her village, she took this child in her arms and ran. Following the Nile, evading enemy guns, shielding the child from looming crocodiles, she had brought him out of those dangers to Egypt. Arriving in Cairo, they stayed in a dangerous slum without work, hoping that one day they finally might find safety and freedom.

I had listened to such stories so many times — stories of flights to refugee camps and slums in foreign lands. Stories of mothers and fathers clinging to their babies and surviving all odds because of the human need to protect the innocence held in their arms. Like the Sudanese mother, Mary and Joseph also ran to Egypt. In an alien land they became refugees — an unwelcomed burden.

Spiritual Exercise

God's ways are not our ways. God's will brings both happiness and trouble. We have children, and they give us so much joy — and so much trouble! When we do a kindness we are at the same time admired — and belittled. Loving one another, we feel both elation and pain.

As you consider the mystery of the flight into Egypt, ponder the moments of exile in your own life. When have you felt ostracized or belittled because of your faith? What good in your life came out of this exile?

5 Finding Comfort in our Sorrow

Standing near the cross of Jesus were his mother, and his mother's sister, Mary the wife of Clopas, and Mary Magdalene. When Jesus saw his mother and the disciple whom he loved standing beside her, he said to his mother, "Woman, here is your son." Then he said to the disciple, "Here is your mother."

John 19:25-27

With the same faith, Mary followed the Lord in his preaching and remained with him all the way to Golgotha.

Door of Faith 13

Sometimes life takes us places where we never thought we would go. The visitors waiting in long lines for clearance outside prison gates never set out to put themselves in such straits. How did their son, daughter, husband, wife end up in this place? They endure the trouble of indignity, of interrogation, of personal searches in order to be with the one they love.

Jesus brought Mary a lot of trouble, yet Mary stayed with him through it all. Her unconditional love endured even in the face of a horrifying sentence — a torturous death on the cross. Although others mocked and tormented him, even as he hung condemned, in her heart Mary pondered the wonder of her son's birth and life. When it was time to say "good-bye," Mary's heart had reached its breaking point. Hardly able to pull himself up to speak, Jesus placed her in the care of the disciple he loved. He did not leave his mother, a widow, alone.

During the rest of her earthly life John cared for Mary, who through the authority of her son's dying wish became the mother of the "Jesus movement." As our mother, as mother of the church, Mary guides us in our suffering and comforts us with her companionship.

Spiritual Exercise

Nothing in the baptism ceremony promises Christians a life free of sorrow. In fact, we are promised the opposite. We follow the one who was crucified for us and, through baptism, are invited to share in both his death and resurrection.

The early church did instruct those who were too enthusiastic to avoid suffering and martyrdom if they could; nevertheless, the early fathers themselves frequently had to confront suffering. Today, ponder the suffering in your own life. What does God say to this suffering? How does God desire to comfort and care for you in your sorrow?

6 Enjoying Resurrected Comfort

For the Mighty One has done great things for me, and holy is his name.

Luke 1:49

By faith, Mary tasted the fruits of Jesus' resurrection.

Door of Faith 13

One year I was fortunate enough to be in Assisi at Eastertime. I kept hearing people talking about the mystery of Jesus meeting Mary after the resurrection — not an episode mentioned in the New Testament, but a scenario planted deep within Mediterranean spirituality. Southern Europeans are convinced that after his resurrection, Jesus would certainly have appeared first to his mother, Mary.

Early before the Easter morning liturgy at Santa Maria degli Angeli in lower Assisi, the mystery of Jesus meeting Mary after the resurrection was celebrated. I, with hundreds of others, walked to the square. Coming down from the upper town, I passed through fields of budding poppies in the lovely morning sun. In the square I waited with the others, who were whispering under their breaths in palpable expectation.

Finally two confraternities, one of men and the other of women, one in red, the other in blue, appeared on opposite sides of the square. They processed with large statues, the red carrying the resurrected Jesus, the blue Mary. In silence the processions inched toward each other until they finally met. With Mary facing Jesus they genuflected with respect toward each. At this, women in the crowd began to weep; even some men wiped away a tear. Following Mary and Jesus, the confraternities processed into the basilica and the crowd followed to begin the Easter celebration.

Spiritual Exercise

Christianity exists because early Christians believed that Jesus rose from the dead. Mediterranean Christians are certain that Jesus would have appeared first to his mother. Why does the Bible not mention this? Perhaps mere words could not describe this story — this mother embracing her beloved son who was dead and now is living. Only the look of love and tears in the eyes of mother and son alike could capture it.

Keeping in mind the sorrow that you identified yesterday, ask Mary and Jesus to embrace you in their resurrected joy. Stay in their embrace, saying nothing by way of explanation, only experiencing the peace of being in the presence of those who truly understand your sorrow.

7

Gathering all in Prayer with Mary

When they entered the city they went to the upper room where they were staying, Peter and John and James and Andrew, Philip and Thomas, Bartholomew and Matthew, James son of Alpha-eus, Simon the Zealot, and Judas son of James. All these were constantly devoting themselves to prayer, together with certain women, including Mary the mother of Jesus, as well as his brothers.

Acts 1:13-14

Treasuring every memory in her heart, she passed them on to the Twelve assembled with her in the Upper Room to receive the Holy Spirit.

Door of Faith 13

Visiting the south for the first time, an African American man was horrified to see evidence of the enormous wealth that had been generated on the backs of slaves. Suddenly beside himself with unanticipated anger, he shared his feelings with an elderly southern woman, also African American. She looked at him and said, "You look for the bad, and are horrified. I prefer to see the good. In every situation, there is good."

This woman's outlook was simple but pro-found. She does not turn herself inside out trying to "forgive her enemy." She has not separated the human race into persecutor and persecuted. Instead, she understands that life has both the positive and the negative. Instead of focusing on evil, she determined to appreciate grace. She had fallen in love with love. For her, everything else was a distraction.

Spiritual Exercise

Below the cross, Mary's heart was completely broken with sorrow. Her beloved child was hanging, writhing in torture, and she could do nothing about it. When her son died, his body was fortunately taken down rather than left for scavengers. Most painfully, the very friends who had promised to remain with her beloved son until the end had abandoned him.

After Jesus' resurrection and ascension, Mary joined these same apostles in prayer. Rather than blame them or harbor anger against them, she recognized their weakness and prayed with them.

We say, "Holy Mary, Mother of God, pray for us sinners." When we join in prayer with Mary, we do not separate humankind into good and bad, perfect and imperfect, saints and sinners. We are all sinners who need Mary as our Mother.

As you pray today, gather the sorrows, loneliness, and joys of your heart and pray, like a mantra, "Holy Mary, Mother of God, pray for us sinners." Repeat this heartfelt prayer over and over, bringing in prayer all those you know before Mary.

Our Evangelizing Mission

four

1 Discerning our Faith Witness

What good is it, my brothers and sisters, if you say you have faith but do not have works? Can faith save you? If a brother or sister is naked and lacks daily food, and one of you says to them, "Go in peace; keep warm and eat your fill," and yet you do not supply their bodily needs, what is the good of that? So faith by itself, if it has no works, is dead.

James 2:14-17

The celebration of faith gives us the opportunity to intensify the witness of charity.

Door of Faith 14

In my senior theology classes at the university, I spend one day on the topic of faith in action. Most of my students agree with St. James: "Faith by itself, if it has no works is dead." They want their Christianity to make a difference within the world.

Generally, we do not ask ourselves if we want to put our faith into action; rather, we ask ourselves how we can do it. We often feel as though whatever we might do is insignificant, that our actions might not present a worthy witness. We get busy with our own lives, detaching ourselves from those who are truly needy and hungry. We give a dollar here and there, but otherwise are disaffected.

I have found that if students study models of ordinary people really responding to the world's poor, they can then identify their own potential contribution. Some people work through nonprofits, some through solidarity by living and being with the poor. Others are involved in education, still others through working with investments and funding for worthy causes. Some spend their energies trying to promote structural change, while others offer themselves as companions to those whose capacity for change is limited — the elderly, addicted, or disabled. All these gifts are witnesses to faith, we need only to express the gift of faith that God has given us.

Spiritual Exercise

No person changes the world alone. If as individuals, however, Christians respond to their gift of faith, the world will change. We need to be humble enough to understand that one person's effort may be insignificant, but that our communal effort is transformative. We also need to understand that God invites our faith and action according to the gifts given us.

Today, spend a few minutes reflecting on your particular gift for reaching out to others. What form does it take — compassion, teaching, healing, administrating, companionship, funding? Today, make a conscious effort to use your gift in the world. Claim this gift and unite it in prayer to building God's communion on earth.

2 Living Faith in Love

But someone will say, "You have faith and I have works." Show me your faith apart from your works, and I by my works will show you my faith. For just as the body without the spirit is dead, so faith without works is also dead.

James 2:18, 26

Faith without charity bears no fruit, while charity without faith is a sentiment constantly at the mercy of doubt.

Door of Faith 14

A phenomenon in religion has been the divide between those who give priority to works and those who give priority to faith. In the church, those who argue to protect and support faith in the form of the institutional church are labeled "conservatives"; those who emphasize works in the form of social action are labeled "liberals." While tension between such perspectives is natural and in some sense healthy, attempting to alienate and discredit others by labeling them is unedifying. We do not build up the body of Christ by tearing each other apart.

Christians need a strong institution that supports faith, provides ministers, baptizes and educates children, blesses marriages, and prays for the dead. We need strong fiscal management, protection for our children, and solid preaching.

On the other hand, a well-managed, believing church without loving action is self-serving and lifeless. True faith demands outreach to the most needy and vulnerable. The dichotomy between faith and works is false. True faith must be expressed in loving outreach.

Spiritual Exercise

Today, try to imagine writing your own creed. As a Christian, what do you truly believe? Why? Why does your belief make a difference? If you had to complete the creedal formula, "I believe in _____," how would you fill in the blank? Perhaps you will say, "I believe in God," or "I believe in Jesus." Perhaps you might answer, "I believe in love," or "I believe in the Trinity." Perhaps important to you is the statement, "I believe that Jesus Christ died and rose," or "I believe that Mary is the Mother of God." Try to identify two or three creedal statements that summarize what is most important to your faith.

Next, ask yourself how you live this faith. If you say that you believe in God, do others see this? Do you live this gift of faith in the world? Does your belief in Jesus or in Mary, the Mother of God, make any difference in your daily life? As you live today, try to be aware of this integration of faith and love in your daily life.

3 Responding to the Beatitudes

Then the king will say to those at his right hand, "Come, you that are blessed by my Father, inherit the kingdom prepared for you from the foundation of the world; for I was hungry and you gave me food, I was thirsty and you gave me something to drink, I was a stranger and you welcomed me, I was naked and you gave me clothing, I was sick and you took care of me, I was in prison and you visited me.

And the king will answer them, "Truly I tell you, just as you did it to one of the least of these who are members of my family, you did it to me."

Matthew 25:34-36, 40

Many Christians dedicate their lives with love to those who are lonely, marginalized, or excluded. These persons demand our attention and support for in them one can see Christ's own face.

Door of Faith 14

We need to be humble in our personal expectations for changing the world. Matthew's Gospel outlines the program in simple terms. We need to feed the hungry, give drink to the thirsty, welcome the stranger, clothe the naked, visit the imprisoned — to provide for those who lack what we have been given.

Yet many of us live comfortable lives and frankly do not know anyone personally who is hungry, without clothes, or imprisoned. While we may struggle to make a living and to provide for our needs, we and those with whom we socialize manage to be self-sufficient. We work hard for our living, and expect that others should also. Because our circumstances may have presented us with only a limited experience of the unfortunate and their personal needs, we may find it difficult to have empathy for those who beg from us.

Although we are willing to follow this gospel mandate, it is difficult to discern how. We do not want to enable those who are lazy or make poor choices. We want to give to those who are truly poor through no fault of their own. We want to follow the gospel wisely.

St. Therese of Lisieux also felt overwhelmed with how she might respond to the call of the gospel. She saw herself as a small person, someone who could do only little things in a complex world. She discerned that her call would be to do what she could at every moment, rather than looking for a big cause — her "little way." Perhaps this "little way" is the path that most of us are called to follow.

Spiritual Exercise

As you make your way through the day, think about Therese of Lisieux's "little way." Are there people in your life who are lonely, need words of encouragement, are hungry for attention, or could use some mentoring? Is there real hunger and nakedness not far from your home? What can you do to make a small difference in your world today?

4 Speaking with Your Soul

But, in accordance with his promise, we wait for new heavens and a new earth, where righteousness is at home. Therefore, beloved, while you are waiting for these things, strive to be found by him at peace, without spot or blemish; and regard the patience of our Lord as salvation.

2 Peter 3:13-15

Supported by faith, let us look with hope at our commitment in the world as we await new heavens and a new earth in which righteousness dwells.

Door of Faith 14

The golden rule says, "Love your neighbor as yourself." Christians place great emphasis on the love of neighbor. We run charities to care for the poor, we sponsor hospitals to nurse the sick, and we pay for schools to educate the young.

But the golden rule has a second part — we are to love our neighbor *as ourselves*. Many times Christians love their neighbor — taking care of the young, providing for the poor, nursing the sick — but fail to care truly for themselves. We somehow imagine that self-care is selfishness. We think that we should be severe to ourselves, but loving toward our neighbor.

The Christian tradition of asceticism seems to support such a harsh notion of spirituality. Yet, such a supposition does not take into account the reality that most ascetics mellow as they grow older, coming to understand how deeply they are loved by God, and by their neighbor. We too are called to be tender to ourselves, to encourage our souls in goodness, and to appreciate ourselves as we have been lovingly created by God.

As she was dying, St. Clare of Assisi said: "I praise and thank you, God, for having created me!" Clare was not self-absorbed; she cherished deeply the precious soul that God had given her. Our mission is to love others *as* we love ourselves. Loving and cherishing our own soul is therefore a measure of our capacity to love the souls of others. As St. Peter says, we are "to be at peace with God." We find this peace when we are at home with God's most precious gift to us — our own soul.

Spiritual Exercise

Today, spend a few minutes speaking with your own soul. What do you usually say to yourself? Are your words and thoughts negative, discouraging, self-degrading? Or are they positive and encouraging?

Next, ask God to speak with your soul. How does God talk with you? Are God's words negative, discouraging, and degrading; or tender, caring, and affirming? As you go about your day, try to relate to your own soul as God does.

Recognizing the Risen Jesus

When he was at the table with them, he took bread, blessed and broke it, and gave it to them. Then their eyes were opened, and they recognized him; and he vanished from their sight. They said to each other, "Were not our hearts burning within us while he was talking to us on the road, while he was opening the scriptures to us?"

That same hour they got up and returned to Jerusalem; and they found the eleven and their companions gathered together. They were saying, "The Lord has risen indeed, and he has appeared to Simon!" Then they told what had happened on the road, and how he had been made known to them in the breaking of the bread.

Luke 24:30-35

Through faith, we can recognize the face of the risen Lord in those who ask for our love.

Door of Faith 14

"Breaking of the bread" is a biblical expression that describes the blessing with which a Jewish meal began, followed by distribution of the bread. Such a blessing included everything that those at the table were sharing. At the Last Supper, however, Jesus used a unique blessing over the bread which was broken and the wine which was shared: "This is my body; this is my blood."

Sometimes the risen Christ appears at our door but we do not recognize him. Perhaps he comes as an in-law who tests our patience. Perhaps Christ is a boss who demands more and more, even while belittling our work. Perhaps he comes as a needy but dirty school child. Such "comings" make it difficult for us to recognize Christ. There seems to be a "great chasm" between us and the very God we love.

God asks us to "love our neighbor as ourselves." When it is difficult to love the most vulnerable of our neighbors — and those are the situations where the risen Lord is most likely to be found — we must consider how we would like to be regarded if we were in their place. If we can love and accept ourselves in such a situation, we may be able to accept and love the risen Lord as he appears in our world.

Spiritual Exercise

Today, consider those you find most difficult to love. Is it someone close to you who tries your patience? Is there a group of people that tests the limits of your Christian faith and care? Is there a physical chasm that you rarely cross in your life: a certain street, a neighborhood, a social boundary?

Try crossing one of those boundaries. Drive into a neighborhood you usually avoid and take a look at the faces of those who live there. Call, write, or talk to someone who you habitually avoid. Read and become more informed about a class of people from whom you generally try to distance yourself.

7 Following the Spirit's Lead

Be careful then how you live, not as unwise people but as wise, making the most of the time, because the days are evil. So do not be foolish, but understand what the will of the Lord is. Do not get drunk with wine, for that is debauchery; but be filled with the Spirit, as you sing psalms and hymns and spiritual songs among yourselves, singing and making melody to the Lord in your hearts, giving thanks to God the Father at all times and for everything in the name of our Lord Jesus Christ.

Ephesians 5:15-20

Intent on gathering the signs of the times in the present of history, faith commits every person to become a living sign of the presence of the risen Lord in the world.

Door of Faith 15

Paul's letter to the Ephesians asks us to live as wise people. We are called to open ourselves to God's action in the world, always seeking to make the most of the opportunities we find. Christians are not called to rant against evil, but to search for the good and follow the Spirit's lead.

As we do our best to be persons who love, we gather with others who also are seeking the Spirit's lead. Since God is love, we know that we are following God when in our day-to-day experience we grasp every opportunity to act with tenderness, compassion, and kindness. With God's living word on our lips and in our hearts, we give praise because our eyes have been opened to seeing the risen Christ walking with us.

How sad it would be if Christians, who believe in the resurrection, lived as though they were passing through life alone. If we walk through our world with Christ, we are always with the God we love, and God is always with us. This "seeing" the risen Christ among us is our wisdom, our happiness, our glory.

Spiritual Exercise

Jesus promised that he would send the Spirit to lead and guide us. Today, open your eyes to the Spirit working within your world. Where do you find opportunities for goodness, for care, for peace? Are you blocked by frustration, darkness, and negativity, or are you following the opportunities that the Spirit offers?

Today, try to make some subtle changes that open you up to happiness and joy. Take a noon walk, listen more carefully to a child, love a spouse more tenderly. Christ is with us, but needs our hands, feet, and hearts to be present within the world. Follow the Spirit's lead and see how Christ becomes present for you and through you.

Also available in the same series:

Forgiveness
*Three Minute Reflections on Redeeming Life's
Most Difficult Moments*
Joan Mueller
ISBN: 978-1-56548-426-9

His Mass and Ours
Meditations on Living Eucharistically
Brendan Leahy
ISBN: 978-1-56548-448-1

Praying Advent
*Three Minute Reflections on Peace, Faithfulness, Joy,
and Light*
Joan Mueller
ISBN: 978-1-56548-358-3

Keepsakes for the Journey
Four Weeks on Faith Deepening
Susan Muto
ISBN: 978-1-56548-333-0

Pathways to Relationship
Four Weeks on Simplicity, Gentleness, Humility, Friendship
Robert F. Morneau
ISBN: 978-1-56548-317-0

Pathways to God
Four Weeks on Faith, Hope and Charity
Robert F. Morneau
ISBN: 978-1-56548-286-9

Those friends on the road to Emmaus did not recognize the body of the risen Jesus immediately, not until he used this unique blessing. What helped them recognize Jesus was not his physical appearance but his word to them and his prayer over the meal they shared.

Spiritual Exercise

Even his closest friends did not recognize the risen Jesus. Mary Magdalene identified him only when he spoke her name. The disciples on the road to Emmaus did not recognize him until the breaking of the bread. As Christians we believe that the risen Jesus is alive with us. How often do we meet him in our daily lives?

To see the face of the risen Jesus we must learn to open our eyes, to recognize him. During his life on earth, Christ appeared in unexpected guises. He arrived as a poor baby born in a manger — in the slums, one might say today. Christ spread God's message not as a Temple priest but as an itinerant preacher. Convicted as an enemy of the state, Christ was executed in the brutal manner reserved for the worst criminals. To find Christ, our eyes must be opened.

As you walk through your world today, ask for the grace to recognize the risen Christ. At the end of the day, ask yourself where you have met him. When was your heart burning within you as you met Christ along your way?

6 Loving our Neighbor as Ourselves

There was a rich man who was dressed in purple and fine linen and who feasted sumptuously every day. And at his gate lay a poor man named Lazarus, covered with sores, who longed to satisfy his hunger with what fell from the rich man's table; even the dogs would come and lick his sores. The poor man died and was carried away by the angels to be with Abraham.

The rich man also died and was buried. In Hades, where he was being tormented, he looked up and saw Abraham far away with Lazarus by his side. He called out, "Father Abraham, have mercy on me, and send Lazarus to dip the tip of his finger in water and cool my tongue; for I am in agony in these flames." But Abraham said, "Child, remember that during your lifetime you received your good things, and Lazarus in like manner evil things; but now he is comforted here, and you are in agony. Besides all this, between you and us a great chasm has been fixed, so that those who might want to pass from here to you cannot do so, and no one can cross from there to us."

Luke 16:19-26

It is faith that enables us to recognize Christ and it is his love that impels us to assist him whenever he becomes our neighbor along the journey of life.

Door of Faith 14